JOYCE HUGGETT

Waiting & Watching

A reflective group study course
for Advent to Epiphany

kevin
mayhew

The publishers wish to express their gratitude to the following for permission to include copyright material in this book:

Concordia Publishing House, 3558 South Jefferson Avenue, St Louis, MO 63118-3968, USA, for the extract from *Finding the Lost: Cultural Keys to Luke 15* (pp. 110, 164), Kenneth Bailey © 1992 Concordia Publishing House.

HarperCollins Publishers Inc, 10 East 53rd Street, New York, NY10022-5299, USA, for the extract from *When the Heart Waits* by Sue Monk Kidd, p. 25 (Harper San Francisco 1990).

Lion Publishing plc, Peter's Way, Sandy Lane West, Oxford, OX4 6HG, for the extract from *The Book of God* by Walter Wangerin, pp. 597-599 (Lion 1996).

HarperCollins Publishers, 77-85 Fulham Palace Road, London, W6 8JB, for the extract from *Celtic Daily Prayer* (from the Northumbria Community). © 2000 The Northumbria Community Trust.

SPCK, Holy Trinity Church, Marylebone Road, London, NW1 4DU, for the extract beginning 'I open the stable door . . .' by David Adam. Also for the extract from *The Coming of God* by Maria Boulding, pp. 39-40 (SPCK 1982).

Illustrations: Joan Hutson: Candle in wreath – p. 6, Path and mountains – p. 37; Sr Elizabeth Ruth Obbard: Return of the prodigal – p. 18; Community of the Holy Cross: Holly – p. 31; Sr Theresa Margaret CHN: Praying hands – p. 28, Joseph – p. 43, Angel and shepherds – p. 53, Mary, Jesus and sheep – p. 55, Crib and star – p. 60, Candle – p. 63, Visit of the magi – p. 68, Advent wreath – pp. 22, 29, 38, 46; Mandy Patterson: Simeon and Jesus – p. 77.

First published in 2002 by KEVIN MAYHEW LTD
Buxhall, Stowmarket, Suffolk IP14 3BW
E-mail: info@kevinmayhewltd.com

© 2002 Joyce Huggett

9 8 7 6 5 4 3 2 1
ISBN 1 84003 950 7
Catalogue No. 1500528

Cover design by Jonathan Stroulger
Edited by Katherine Laidler
Typeset by Louise Selfe
Printed and bound in Great Britain

For Dianne
With love and thanks

Contents

Acknowledgements

Behind every book that is published hides not just an author but a whole team of people. As *this* book goes to print, I'd like to thank publicly some members of 'my' team.

First, my thanks go to my publisher, Kevin Mayhew, who has not only given me the privilege of producing this material but, by his kindness, courtesy and encouragement, has also cheered me on each step of the way.

Next, my thanks go to my editor, Katherine Laidler, whose gentle encouragement and astute editing have left me feeling affirmed and excited at the thought of groups of people using the material that has evolved through our partnership.

The third member of the Kevin Mayhew team to whom I am indebted is Kevin Whomes, whose cheerful, caring, practical, down-to-earth help energised me in such a way that I found myself enjoying some of the tasks that I normally find irksome and tiring.

I have not yet had the pleasure of meeting any of these people but already I feel they are my friends.

My husband read and reread the manuscript as it evolved and, as always, made invaluable observations and suggestions for which I am truly grateful.

As for Dianne, to whom this small book is dedicated, I remember with joy the enthusiasm with which she read the early, raw pages of the manuscript. Her enthusiasm in watching the material evolve and her desire to see the booklet in print, as well as her practical help here in our home, spurred me on when energy levels dropped.

Last, but by no means least, I send a wave of thanks to two other groups of friends. First, the four artists who have kindly and generously permitted me to use their powerful illustrations. Second, the many who have prayed for me while this booklet was being born including, in particular, my Spiritual Director whose love and wisdom and gentle challenge helped to keep me focused on the One on whom groups who use this book will focus: God – Father, Son and Holy Spirit.

Introduction

'We've almost exhausted the material I've prepared for our group meetings and it will soon be Advent. Does anyone know of any Advent material we could use?' That's the question the leader of a certain house group put to his group members in the middle of November last year.

A few days after someone from that group told me the story, I received a letter from Kevin Mayhew inviting me to write some material that members of such groups could use. I had just completed the manuscript of a book of Advent, Christmas and Epiphany meditations for *individuals*[1] so my mind was still fully focused on the wonder of this time of year. At the same time I felt challenged by the expressed need felt by the house group leader I had heard about. So I accepted the publisher's invitation.

I worked on the material for this booklet throughout the Advent/Christmas/ Epiphany season:

- *Advent* which places the spotlight on the second coming of Christ
- *Christmas* with its focus on the first coming into the world of the Christ-child
- *Epiphany* with its emphasis on the good news for those of us who are not of Jewish descent – that Christ came for the *whole world*.

While I was preparing the material for the book, I had in my mind not only groups of people who meet regularly but clusters of three, four or more people who have agreed to meet together for eight weeks from the beginning of Advent to the middle of January or beginning of February. Their specific aim would be to focus on the mysteries that beg to be pondered and prayed with at this time of year but that so easily become overlaid with the busyness that distracts us and steals from us time to contemplate. I also have in mind two other groups: prayer partners who meet regularly and who might appreciate material to help them ponder the wonders in which this time of year is steeped, and young mums. Many young mums find that, when they have small children with them all day and sometimes for part of the night as well, time and energy for prayer seem to evaporate, or, on those rare occasions when an opportunity for prayer, meditation or Bible reading arises, they are too tired to concentrate. At this stage of life, meeting with other young mums can be a great

---

1. Joyce Huggett, *Joy to the World* (Guildford: Eagle, 2001)

encouragement – especially during this season when much of our thinking centres on motherhood and the birth of the Christ-child. I would love to think that members of a church would offer to organise a crèche or to baby-sit so that mums could meet together to enjoy working through this book together as Christmas draws near.

As I wrote, I bore in mind the fact that, for many of us, the mysteries that fill our minds and hearts at this special time of year cannot be confined to *words*. Many people need and are enriched by a multi-media approach:

- visual stimuli like pictures, Advent calendars, Advent wreathes, candles
- audio aids like carols and chants, prayers and poems read or recited
- and, of course, the discussion and sharing that characterise such group gatherings.

For this reason, I suggest that, as each meeting starts, the group leader or another member of the group prepares the meeting room by placing, on a table or on the floor in the centre of the room, an object or picture that will stimulate the group members. This visual aid could be one or more of the following:

- A solitary candle arranged on an attractive cloth or standing in the middle of an Advent wreath.

- An Advent wreath with four candles – one candle to be lighted towards the end of each of the meetings before Christmas.

- A picture or collection of pictures that members of the group bring and that could be made into a collage. The picture could be an enlarged copy of some of the pictures that appear in this book. Most of them look very impressive when enlarged and laminated. Or, as you will see, on some occasions, I have made specific suggestions of picture collections that groups could make.

- An appropriate Christmas card.
- An Advent calendar.
- A Christmas crib. If you use a crib, there are advantages in building up the scene gradually rather than placing a complete manger scene in the room from the first week. Start, perhaps, with a few animals: some

sheep or cows or oxen. Each week add a few more animals or some shepherds or the empty manger. Eventually bring on Mary and Joseph and the donkey. If you introduce the wise men before Christmas, let them stand in line in another part of the room rather than approach the manger early. This means that, near the day when many sections of the Church celebrate the arrival in Bethlehem of the Magi, your wise men can reach your crib.

In addition to some of the above, I am also assuming that a cassette player or CD player will be placed in the meeting room before members of the group arrive.

I have designed the material in such a way that each week, with the exception of the first week, the pattern will be the same:

- First, the leader or another member of the group will help the group members to 'dial down' – to open themselves to receive whatever gift God has prepared for them. I have called this section **Group preparation**, and imagine that, most weeks, this could take between five and fifteen minutes.

- The theme of the week will then be explored by focusing on a passage of Scripture – a section that I have called **Scripture focus**. This section may take a little longer than the first, depending on the length of the Bible passage chosen and the length of the comment that comes with it. The time span should not exceed ten minutes – except in Week 8 when the format of the meeting is slightly different.

- After the Scripture focus, there is a section called **Personal exploration** and **Personal sharing**. The Personal exploration part of this section is intended to give each individual between five and ten minutes to explore and respond to the Bible passage *on their own*. At the end of that time the group moves into Personal sharing. In other words, members of the group will be given a brief opportunity to share with everyone some of the insights that have come to them during this time of reflection. Different people will take varying lengths of time when sharing in this way, so the leader of the group will need to keep a careful eye on the clock and decide, and let group members know beforehand, how much time will be allocated to this important and moving part of the meeting.

The person who leads this part of the meeting may also need to remind the group that the aim of personal sharing is *not* to open up a discussion. It is simply to provide individuals with a chance to say,

'This is what I saw . . .', 'This is what I sense . . .', 'This is what I heard . . .', 'This is what I experienced . . .'. The role of the group is to listen with care and interest and to receive what is shared with no hint of judgement or expressed criticism, and no invitation to the group to comment, except, perhaps, to say thank you to those who have plucked up courage to share in this way. Indeed, it can often be helpful to suggest that, after each person has spoken, the group should remain silent for a few seconds – to ponder, to receive, to reflect, or to pray silently.

- **Group discussion** is scheduled to follow the sharing. Again, the group leader (in consultation with the group) will be the one who decides what proportion of the meeting will be given over to this. For some members of the group, it will be a vital part of the group activity. For others the personal exploration and personal sharing mentioned above will prove to be more valuable. So, perhaps, most groups should aim at a maximum of twenty minutes for this part of the meeting.

- The meeting ends with an invitation to gather up the thoughts and experiences of the time together by listening to music (possibly by candlelight) as well as the opportunity to pray together. I have called this final section **Worship time**, and envisage it taking between ten and fifteen minutes.

You will notice that I have referred several times to 'the group leader'. The material has been arranged in such a way, though, that it would be possible, and probably advisable, for different people to lead different sections of the meeting. Some people, for example, are gifted in leading others into silence and reflection and quiet worship, while others have a gift for reading a Scripture passage aloud in such a way that the Bible really comes alive. Yet others have the kind of sensitivity that encourages group members to share the insights that have come to the surface for them during a period of reflection, while some are more skilled at leading a discussion. If you have been meeting regularly as a group before Advent begins, you will probably already know which people could best lead which parts of the meeting. If you are meeting together for the first time, you will have a more challenging task discerning who will best lead which section. It is possible that the quiet, retiring people who believe they are no good at leading *anything* will, in fact, excel at leading the group into stillness and encouraging group members to share the insights that have come to them during periods of reflection.

While writing this book, I have assumed that each member of the group will have their own copy. This way everyone can read the week's 'programme' before they come to the meeting, during the meeting itself and when they return home.

The title *Waiting and Watching* came to me as the booklet evolved. The material begins by placing the spotlight on the Advent God – the one who watches and waits and yearns for us to return to him. It continues by observing how a variety of people who watched and waited for God responded to and were changed by his presence and love. My prayer is that as groups and individuals use the material, their hearts will be strangely warmed and their heads informed – so much so that they will have no need of the invitation to 'Come and adore him . . . Christ the Lord' because, having met with others in this way, such adoration will be spontaneous and heartfelt – both in the group and at home throughout Advent, Christmas and Epiphany, and on into the challenges another new year will bring.

JOYCE HUGGETT

Week 1

Getting started

Waiting can be exciting. Waiting can be worrying. Waiting can be energising. Waiting can be stressful. It all depends on what you are waiting for, how long you've been waiting and what kind of person you are.

To underline what I mean, I am now going to list some occasions when I have had to wait. I'm going to invite you to imagine how *you* would have felt if you had been in my shoes. The aim of the exercise is simply to remind you that waiting is an important part of life and, because it comes in a variety of disguises, our reactions to it inevitably vary.

- As I write, a friend of mine is undergoing a very serious operation so I am waiting for the phone to ring giving me some news.

    How might you feel if you were in my shoes?

- My much-loved brother emigrated to Australia when I was in my mid-20s. He didn't return to this country for 17 years. Then, one Christmas, he wrote to say he was coming to visit us the following June.

    How might you have felt during that six-month wait if you had been in my shoes?

- When I was in the first year of the sixth-form at school, I received a message from the headmistress. I was to go to her study at 11am. When I knocked at her study door she was busy so she asked me to wait outside for a few minutes.

    How might you have felt about waiting if you had been in my shoes?

- My husband and I work for a missionary organisation. Our role is to provide pastoral care for missionaries and, over the years, it has involved a great deal of travelling. Once, we travelled from Cyprus (where we then lived) to Singapore via the Gulf. When we reached the Gulf, where we had to change planes, we found ourselves stranded. Although we had tickets for the ongoing journey, we discovered that the flight had been over-booked and that we and 18 other passengers were refused permission to board the plane to Singapore. We had to wait for 12 hours before we *could* board a plane.

    How might you have felt if you had been in our shoes?

- On one of my trips overseas I bought a Christmas present for a friend. I wrapped it up on Christmas Eve. As I did so, I kept saying to myself,

'I can't wait to see her face when she opens it!' On Christmas Day I gave her the present.

How might you have felt as you waited and watched her open the parcel?

Your turn

You have heard a little bit about my experience of waiting. Now it is your turn!

Divide the group into sub-groups of not more than three people in each group. Invite each person to tell a brief story of an occasion when he or she had to wait for something or someone. Invite each person to explain how they felt while they were waiting.

When each person has told their story, ask someone from each group to volunteer to be the spokesperson. Then invite each group to draw up a statement that lists some of the emotions that people experience when they have to wait:

Waiting can be . . .
....
....
....
....
....
....
....

When each sub-group has completed their list, invite the spokesperson to read out the emotions expressed so that a whole variety of feelings is spread before the entire group. Then ask someone to volunteer to read the following quotation to the whole group:

Advent is the consecration of waiting in our lives. Human life is full of waiting: people wait for trains, buses and planes; they stand in queues at shops; they sit nervously in dentists' waiting-rooms; they wait in anguish for news of a lost loved one. They wait for the slow process of healing to take its time; they wait for the birth of a child. Waiting can be very different in these different situations, according to our attitude. In an age of 'instant' products any delay can be viewed as negative, for 'time is money'. Yet some things cannot be skimped or hurried; we have to let them take the time they need. You can't make the grass grow by pulling it, as the proverb wisely warns. . . . Faith can demand long, patient waiting when nothing seems to be happening, and this is . . . necessary to growth. . . . The waiting changes us, schools us, teaches us to know God:

> The Lord waits to be gracious to you . . .
> Blessed are all those who wait for him.
> *Isaiah 30:18*[1]

Against this backcloth of our own experiences of and feelings about waiting, and this claim that Advent is 'the consecration of waiting in our lives', we now move into the first session. As we do so, I am wondering whether anyone admitted that waiting can be agony because that is the title for Week 1.

---

1. Maria Boulding, *The Coming of God* (London: SPCK, 1982) pp. 39-40

Agonised waiting

Waiting can be agony. As I write, the parents, teachers and friends of an attractive teenager wait for news of the whereabouts of this 13-year-old who disappeared ten days ago. Their distress reminds me of the vicar's wife who once poured out her pain to me. Her daughter had not been abducted. She had just left home of her own premeditated free will. She left for school one morning but didn't return that evening. A few weeks later she telephoned to assure her parents that she was still alive but she became one of the world's 'lost' children who choose to disappear in the anonymity of a big city.

Jesus once told a story about a man who had two 'lost' sons. He told the story, not to place the spotlight on the sons but rather to spell out the amazing news that God his Father is like the father in the story.

Scripture focus

There was a man who had two sons; and the younger of them said to his father, 'Father! Give me the share of the property that will belong to me.' And he divided his property between them. Not many days later the younger son sold all he had, travelled to a distant country, and wasted his property in extravagant living. And when he had spent everything, a severe famine took place in that country and he began to be in need.

So he went and joined himself to one of the citizens of that country. And he sent him to his field to feed the pigs. And he would gladly have filled himself with the pods that the pigs were eating, and no one gave him anything. And when he came to himself he said, 'How many of my father's craftsmen have bread enough and to spare, but here I am dying of hunger! I will arise and go to my father and say to him, "Father, I have sinned against heaven and before you and am not now worthy to be called your son. Fashion out of me a craftsman."' And he arose and came to his father.

And while he was still at a great distance, his father saw him and had compassion and ran and fell upon his neck and kissed him. And the son said to the father, 'Father, I have sinned against heaven and before you and am not now worthy to be called your son.' And the father said to the servants, 'Bring quickly the best robe and put it on him, and put a ring on his hands and sandals on his feet; and bring the fatted calf and kill it, and let us eat and celebrate, for this my son was dead and is alive, he was lost and is found.' And they began to celebrate.

Now the elder son was in the field, and when he came and approached the house, he heard music and dancing. And he called one of the boys and asked what this meant. And he said to him, 'Your brother has come, and your father has killed the fatted calf because he recovered him with peace.' Then he became angry and refused to go in.

So his father came out and began to plead with him. But he answered his father, 'Listen, for all these years, I have been working like a slave for you, and I never disobeyed your commandments, yet you never gave me even a young goat so that I might celebrate with my friends. But when this son of yours came back, who has devoured your living with prostitutes, you killed the fatted calf for him!'

And the father said to him, 'Beloved son, you are always with me, and all that is mine is yours. And to celebrate and rejoice was necessary, for this brother was dead and has come to life, he was lost and has been found.'

[And the older son embraced his father and entered the house and was reconciled to his brother and to his father. And the father celebrated together with his two sons.]

Luke 15:11-32[1]

Comment

This story that reminds us that the God of Advent is a God who waits and watches can only really be understood when we place it in its Middle Eastern context. Through his books and sermons and talks, Professor Kenneth Bailey, whose translation of the parable you have just read, has helped us to do this. As Professor Bailey translates the beginning of the parable:

> There was a man who had two sons; and the younger of them said to his father, 'Father! Give me the share of the property that will belong to me.' And he divided his property between them.

When we place the story in its Middle Eastern context, it quickly becomes apparent that what the young man was saying, by implication, was, 'Father, I wish you would drop dead so that I could have my inheritance NOW.'[2]

---

1. Professor Kenneth Bailey's translation in *Finding the Lost: Cultural Keys to Luke 15* (St Louis: Concordia 1992) pp. 110, 164
2. *ibid.*

'What would *you* do if your son said that to you?' I asked a group of Singaporean Church leaders on one occasion. 'I'd kick him out' was the angry, spontaneous response of one of the men.

The father in Jesus' story did not kick his son out of the home. He acted very differently. He did what his son demanded. He gave him his inheritance and he watched while his son packed his bag and set off for a distant country. His watching did not cease when the figure of his restless son disappeared over the horizon. The watching led to a prolonged period of waiting. The father knew his son well enough to feel certain that, one day, he would return. The father also knew that, unless he greeted his son first on his return to their village, his boy would be *unable* to come back because, if ever a villager left the village in such circumstances, a cutting-off ceremony was performed by the village elders. When the villager was cut off it meant that he was no longer considered to be a citizen of the village and would not be allowed on village soil again.

With this in mind the father watched and waited and waited some more. Jesus does not provide us with a time scale so we have no idea how long he waited but the implication is that it was months or even years rather than merely a few weeks. We can only imagine the agony this father went through as, day by day, he endured this seemingly never-ending vigil.

Eventually, his waiting was rewarded. As Jesus describes that unforgettable moment:

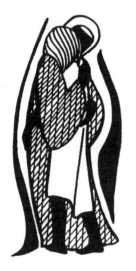

When he was a long way off,
his father saw him,
was filled with compassion for him,
ran to him,
threw his arms around him
and kissed him.

What a welcome! Try to picture the scene. Men in the Middle East, as we are reminded when we see them on our television screens, dress in long, flowing robes. Such robes make running almost impossible – unless the wearer does something that is culturally unacceptable and therefore unthinkable: gathering up his skirts and showing his legs. Yet, the father in Jesus' story *ran*. The implication is that he *raced* through the narrow streets to the very edge of the village to welcome his boy home. Streets in those days were made just wide enough for one person riding a donkey bearing well-laden sidesaddles, so it was not an easy feat to run through the village.

The sight of the racing father would have been so curious and so scandalous that the whole village would have pursued him to discover the reason for this outrageous behaviour. So the father's embrace and welcome on the outskirts of the village would have been witnessed by most if not all of the villagers. They would have seen the father's kiss, felt his compassion, witnessed the son's filthy body being covered by a clean robe, and his tired and torn feet being slipped into sandals. They would have heard and seen the father's delight and his determination to celebrate: 'Let's have a party!' Middle Easterners love parties – the camaraderie, the feasting, the dancing – so all the village would be there when the barbecued beef was ready. Little did they realise, though, that in the middle of that party they would watch this father being plunged into a different kind of waiting.

A different sort of waiting and watching

When the father's eldest son heard the sound of music as he returned home from the fields, the culture demanded that, whether he had been told about the party or not, his role was to go into the house, change into his party clothes, and mingle among the guests with his parents. The elder brother's behaviour in *refusing* to go inside was outrageous. By implication, he was insulting his father and, in the Middle East, this is totally unacceptable. In fact, his behaviour, in some respects, was more damaging to his father than his brother's rejection had been. The younger brother's rejection of his father had at least been played out in private but here was the elder brother insulting his father *in public* – with the whole village looking and listening and absorbing and probably commenting.

If the father had decided to act according to the cultural norm, he would have sent his servants to the courtyard to drag the elder brother into the house and lock him in a room. After the party was over, the elder brother would then have been flogged. *This* father does not do that. For the second time that day, he amazes the villagers by doing what no Middle Eastern father would do. He leaves the party, goes out to the courtyard and *pleads* with his eldest son. By this time, the music and the dancing would have stopped. The party guests would have followed the father out of the house where they could watch and listen to the show-down. So all the guests would have been witnesses to the venom and insults pouring from the eldest son on to his father. They would have also heard the father respond not with the deserved condemnation but with patience, kindness and generosity: '*Beloved son*, all that I have is yours . . .'

Did this son come into the party? That's the cliffhanger on which Jesus ends his story. The three final lines of the parable as it is printed on page 17 sum up the way the father longed that the story would end but, as Ken Bailey rightly reminds us, the only way we will ever know whether or not the elder brother *did* go in with his father is to look at ourselves and to ask:

> Will *I* go into the party or will I stand in the courtyard yelling and screaming at God for the things he has failed to do for me?

Most of us need this annual reminder that the God of Advent is like this father in Jesus' parable. We, God's Advent people, fall into two cate-gories. Some of us are like the younger son. Knowingly, deliberately, we have turned our back on God and have wasted the riches that God has given us. Even more of us are like the elder brother. Dutifully, we have stayed in the church or the fellowship, serving God at great cost to our-selves. As one such person once put it to me: 'I've been so busy *serving* God, I haven't stopped to love him.' Deep down, on such occasions, we may feel frustrated, angry and used. Yet the God of Advent assures each of us that:

> In repentance and rest is your salvation,
> in quietness and trust is your strength . . .
>
> the Lord longs to be gracious to you,
> he rises to show you compassion.
> For the Lord is a God of justice.
> Blessed are all who wait for him!'
> *Isaiah 30:15, 18 (NIV)*

Personal exploration

Invite members of the group to be silent now for several minutes to give each person the opportunity to ask the following question:

- At this moment in time, as I think about my relationship with God, do I feel more like the youngest son or his older brother?

When you have found your answer to that question, ask yourself another:

- Do I know why I feel this way about my relationship with God?
- What would you like to say to the Father? Write a prayer now.

Personal sharing

Invite members of the group to share their responses to the above questions if they would like to.

Group discussion

- How do you imagine the father felt as he waited and watched for the return of his youngest son?
- How do you imagine he felt when he found himself on the receiving end of his elder son's onslaught?
- How do you feel about a father who offers such love to both his children?
- What do you sense Jesus wants us to remember most about this father?

Worship time

- Light *one* candle of the Advent wreath if you have one.

- Listen to the song 'Come back to me'.[1]

- Invite those who would like to to read aloud the prayer that they have written.

- Say the following prayer together:

Waiting,
watching
God,
give us the grace
to respond to your love
and to come to you afresh
today
and
every day.
Amen.

- Listen to the song 'Just as I am'.[2]

Preparing for next week

During the coming week look out for and collect pictures of people in pain, and pictures that symbolise some of the evil in our world. Bring these pictures with you to next week's meeting.

---

1. Marilla Ness, *Come Back to Me* CD and cassette, Merciful Love Music
2. Jane Lilley Singers, *Joy to the World* CD and cassette published by Eagle

Week 2

Eager waiting

Visual focus

At the beginning of the meeting, invite members of the group to lay, on a table or on the floor, the pictures depicting evil and pain that they have brought with them.

Group preparation

- Be still for a few seconds. Become aware of the presence of God in the room where you are meeting. Remind yourself that God is attentive to your longings and your heartaches, so hand them over to him.

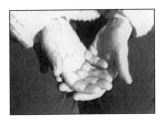

- When you are ready, let your hands lie gently in your lap with your palms turned up as a sign that you are open to receive whatever God wants to give you during this meeting.
- Listen to the chorus 'Spirit of the Living God'[1] or 'Calm me, Lord'[2].

Scripture focus

Now invite someone to read the promise an angel gave as Jesus was ascending into heaven:

> When [Jesus' disciples] were together for the last time they asked, 'Master, are you going to restore the kingdom of Israel now? Is this the time?'
>
> He told them, 'You don't get to know the time. Timing is the Father's business. What you'll get is the Holy Spirit. And when the Holy Spirit comes on you, you will be able to be my witnesses in Jerusalem, all over Judea and Samaria, even to the ends of the world.'
>
> These were his last words. As they watched, he was taken up and disappeared in a cloud. They stood there, staring into the empty sky. Suddenly two men appeared – in white robes! They said, 'You Galileans

1. You can find this song on the *Open to God* cassette published by Eagle
2. You can find this soothing song on the *Fire of Love* CD and cassette by Margaret Rizza, published by Kevin Mayhew, and also on the *Joy to the World* CD and cassette published by Eagle

– why do you just stand here looking up at an empty sky? This very Jesus who was taken up from among you to heaven will come as certainly – and mysteriously – as he left.'
Acts 1:6-9 (The Message)

Comment

This is not the only reference in the Bible to Jesus' return. Peter Johnston claims that 'there are no less than 319 passages in the New Testament which refer directly to the return of the Lord Jesus Christ.'[1]

The book of the Bible that focuses fully on the magnificence of the Returning One is the Book of Revelation. This book begins by painting a picture of the author, John, languishing on the idyllic island of Patmos. There, John had little opportunity to enjoy the stunning beauty of that Greek island because he was imprisoned in a dark and dingy cave near the top of the highest point on the island. His crime? He had been preaching the Gospel. Now, as well as feeling keenly the isolation of imprisonment, he also clearly felt burdened for the churches he pastored. Even so, such is the calibre of this man of God that on the Sabbath Day he was 'in the Spirit'. As Eugene Peterson puts it, on this day John was 'God-intoxicated, God possessed, God-articulate.'[2] In fact, John was so open to God and focused on God that he was given a powerful picture of Jesus, the Son of Man:

 I, John, with you all the way in the trial and the kingdom and the passion of patience in Jesus, was on the island called Patmos because of God's Word, the witness of Jesus. It was Sunday and I was in the Spirit, praying. I heard a loud voice behind me, trumpet-clear and piercing: 'Write what you see into a book. Send it to the seven churches . . .' I turned and saw the voice.

I saw a gold menorah
  with seven branches,
and in the centre, the Son of Man,
  in a robe and gold breastplate,
  hair a blizzard of white,
eyes pouring fire-blaze,

1. The Revd R. Peter Johnston, *Remember, I Am Coming Soon!* (London: Victory Press, 1964) p. 11

2. Eugene Peterson, *Reversed Thunder* (London: HarperCollins, 1988) p. 3

        both feet furnace-fired bronze,
his voice a cataract,
        right hand holding the Seven Stars,
his mouth a sharp-biting sword,
        his face a perigee sun.

I saw this and fainted dead at his feet. His right hand pulled me upright, his voice reassured me:

> 'Don't fear: I am First, I am Last, I'm Alive. I died, but I came to life, and my life is now for ever. See these keys in my hand? They open and lock Death's doors, they open and lock Hell's gates. Now write down everything you see: things that are, things about to be.'

Revelation 1:9-20 (The Message)

As Eugene Peterson reminds us, 'The vision of Christ begins with a description of his clothing: "a long robe with a golden girdle round his breast."' Before we know what the Son of Man looks like, we know what he does because a person's clothing often defines his or her role. So we not only recognise a policeman by his dress, we also know what his role is. The clothing we see the Son of Man wearing tells us immediately that he is a priest. A priest's role is to act as a bridge between God and people. The priest presents people to God and he also presents God to people. In other words, he acts as a go-between, bringing together the divine and the human. This will be Jesus' role when he returns.

Jesus is not only 'the Go-between God', as some Christians like to call him; his snow-white hair reminds us that he is through-and-through pure, while his eyes, like flames of fire, are purifying. Just as fire penetrates and transforms, so Jesus' gaze penetrates and purifies us. 'He doesn't look at us, he looks *into* us.'[1] He invades us, burning up in us all that would prevent us from coming close to him.

He is not only pure and purifying, he has an unforgettable voice that is as striking as the sound of a mighty, majestic waterfall, and the message his voice thunders is one of 'passionate love and urgent mercy'.[2] As to his face, it is not only like the sun when it is shining in full strength, it communicates to each individual who beholds it the joyful message that God waits to be gracious to us. As we are reminded in Numbers 6:25, this face communicates a message of blessing and protection and peace:

---

1. Eugene Peterson, *Reversed Thunder* (London: HarperCollins, 1988) p. 34
2. *ibid.*, p. 39

May the Lord bless you
and protect you.
May the Lord smile on you
and be gracious to you.
May the Lord show you his favour
and give you his peace.
Numbers 6:24-26 (NLT)

In other words, through this vision, John was reminded that God in Christ is warmth and sunlight and that same message is communicated by John to us today.

As though this free-flowing love and mercy, blessing and forgiveness were not enough, the unfolding vision that was given to John reminds us that there is more – much more. When Christ returns, there will be no more pain (Revelation 21:1-4), no more sin (Revelation 21:22-27), no more down-drag from Satan (Revelation 20:1-3; 10). Instead, there will be a grand reunion of those who love God (1 Thessalonians 4:13-15; 17).

As you drink in these promises –

no more pain; no more sin; no more evil –

look at the pictures people brought to the meeting and thank God that, during Advent, we focus not on the present only but also on the fact that a new day is dawning when pain and evil will become terrors of the past.

Matthew Henry once summed up the situation in this way:

The principal happiness of heaven is this, *to be with the Lord,* to see him, live with him, and enjoy him for ever. This should comfort (Christians) upon the death of their friends. We and they . . . shall meet our Lord, and be with him for ever, no more to be separated either from him or from one another for ever.[1]

---

1. Matthew Henry, *Commentary on the Whole Bible* (London: Marshall Morgan and Scott, 1960) p. 678

Personal exploration

Like last week, give everyone time and space now for a few minutes of personal reflection when they can respond by themselves to the following questions:

If Jesus should choose to return today while you are in this meeting:

- How might you react? What might you say? How would you feel?
- Do you know why you would respond in this way?
- Write a prayer to God in the light of what you have just seen and heard and felt.

Personal sharing

Invite members of the group to read aloud part or all of the prayer they have written. Others might prefer to share one of the insights that impressed itself on them as they made their response to God.

Group discussion

- What prevents/dissuades people from doing what Jesus asked us to do – to watch and wait for his second coming?
- Someone has said, 'If you are at times so weary and involved with the struggle of living that you have no strength even to want him, yet you are still dissatisfied that you don't, you are already keeping Advent in your life.'[1] What makes it hard for Christians to believe this good news?
- Christians in the early Church talked often about the second coming of Jesus. Why don't we?

Worship time

- Since this is the second week in Advent, light two candles if you have an Advent wreath.
- As you watch the candles burning, listen to the song 'Like a candle flame'[2].
- Pause to pray for the bereaved, people in pain and victims of evil. One way of doing this is

---

1. Maria Boulding
2. This song may be found on *The Graham Kendrick Collection* CD and cassette published by Kevin Mayhew

to invite group members simply to mention the Christian name of anyone known to them who needs our prayers at this moment in time, and for the group, in the silence, to hold these people into God's love and care.

- Invite one person to read the following Bible verses and suggest that everyone else joins in the refrain, 'Maranatha! Come, Lord Jesus.'[1]

O God, you are my God, for you I long;
for you my soul is thirsting.[2]

> *Maranatha!*
> *Come, Lord Jesus.*

Through the night my soul longs for you,
deep within me my spirit reaches out to you.[3]

> *Maranatha!*
> *Come, Lord Jesus.*

I long for the Lord
more than sentries long for the dawn,
yes, more than sentries long for the dawn . . .[4]

> *Maranatha!*
> *Come, Lord Jesus.*

Hope in the Lord;
for with the Lord there is unfailing love
and an overflowing supply of salvation.[5]

> *Maranatha!*
> *Come, Lord Jesus.*

When the Son of Man comes in his glory,
and all the angels with him,
he will sit on his throne in heavenly glory.[6]

> *Maranatha!*
> *Come, Lord Jesus.*

- Finally, as you listen to the hymn 'I cannot tell'[7], recall some of the insights that have been shared during this meeting and how you have felt about them. Spread these memories and feelings before God.

---

1. The word 'Maranatha' simply means 'come'
2. Psalm 63:2 (Grail translation)
3. Isaiah 26:9 (The Message)
4. Psalm 130:6 (NLT)
5. Psalm 130:7 (NLT)
6. Matthew 25:31 (NIV)
7. This song has been recorded on the *Joy to the World* CD and cassette published by Eagle

Preparing for next week

During the coming week, look and listen carefully for ways in which we are being urged to prepare for Christmas this year. From magazines, flyers and newspapers, cut out advertisements and articles that persuade us that there are certain things we *must* do or certain commodities that we *must* have if our Christmas is to be complete. Bring these pictures with you to next week's meeting. Meanwhile, perhaps one or two people would volunteer to make a collage of the pictures members of the group brought to today's meeting. You could find that, between you, you have made a powerful *Collage of Pain*.

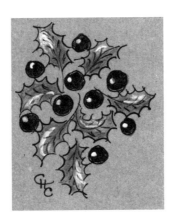

Week 3

Active waiting

Visual focus

At the beginning of the meeting, spread on a table or the floor the pictures, advertisements and articles members of the group have collected from magazines and newspapers this past week.

Group preparation

Jesus once told a story about a farmer who scattered seed on the terraced strip of land that he farmed. Some seed fell on the path where the soil was so hard-packed that the seed had no chance of pushing down roots. Birds swooped on this seed and gobbled it up. Some seed fell among the shoulder-high thistles and weeds that enjoy prolific growth in the part of the world where Jesus was teaching. As soon as these seeds started to grow, their life was choked by these towering plants. Yet other seed fell on stony ground – that is, on the table of solid rock on which top-soil had been spread. Here the soil was so shallow that the roots had no chance of burrowing deep enough into good, rich, fertile soil. These seeds, too, shrivelled and died. Some seed, though, fell on good, rich, fertile pockets of soil. This seed grew and bore plentiful and welcome fruit.

When the disciples asked Jesus why he told stories like this, Jesus replied, 'To create readiness . . . To nudge the people toward receptive insight.'[1] As this meeting begins, ask yourself what kind of soil your heart is like at this moment in time:

- Hard-packed because of busyness, bitterness, resentment, frustration?

- Stony because you are harbouring hard or harsh attitudes towards others?

- Closed to God's voice because the weeds of worry strangle the life-giving Word of God?

- Fertile because your heart is ready to receive God's Word afresh?

Write a prayer or draw a picture or diagram that sums up how you feel as this meeting begins. If you feel you can, finish the prayer by asking God to create inside you a heart-readiness to receive anything he wants to give you during this meeting. Or echo this prayer:

---

1. Matthew 13:13 (The Message). For a fuller explanation of this story told by Jesus, see Joyce Huggett, *Hearing Jesus* (Eagle, 1999)

Lord, you came to create heart-readiness.
May my heart be so like fertile soil
that your Word takes root in it,
pushes up shoots from it
and bears much fruit for you.

Scripture focus

One Saturday, after I had spent the morning mulling over the insights I wanted to share with you for this week's meeting, the phone rang. The friend on the other end of the line simply said, 'I'd love to see you. Is it all right if I come round for an hour?' I said that I'd enjoy having her in my home and suggested that, since my husband was away, she and I should have supper together. So my waiting for her arrival proved to be extremely active. I wanted the salad supper to be ready before she arrived.

One of the key players in the drama of the first Advent is one whose slogan – 'Prepare the way of the Lord'– urges us at this time of year to ensure that our waiting for God is active rather than passive:

> There was once a man, his name John, sent by God to point out the way to the Life-Light. He came to show everyone where to look, who to believe in. John was not himself the Light; he was there to show the way to the Light . . .
>
> The Word became flesh and blood,
>   and moved into the neighbourhood.
> We saw the glory with our own eyes,
>   the one-of-a-kind glory,
>   like Father, like Son,
>   generous inside and out,
>   true from start to finish.
>
> John pointed him out and called, 'This is the One! The One I told you was coming after me but in fact was ahead of me. He has always been ahead of me, has always had the first word . . . *Make the road straight for God!*'
> *John 1:6-8; 15, 23 (The Message)*

John the Baptist was echoing words that had first been penned by the Prophet Isaiah:

Prepare the way of the Lord;
make straight in the wilderness
a highway for our God.
Every valley shall be raised up,
every mountain and hill made low;
the rough ground shall become level,
the rugged places a plain.
And the glory of the Lord will be revealed,
and all mankind together will see it.
For the mouth of the Lord has spoken.
Isaiah 40:3-5 (NIV)

Comment

Like John the Baptist, we can prepare the way of the Lord in these days leading up to Christmas. As someone has helpfully expressed it:

> Being ready for Christmas should mean that our thoughts are focused not just on letters and cards, shopping and presents, but on repentance, humbling and interior 'housecleaning'. John the Baptist warned his hearers to prepare a way for the Lord – to make a clear and level pathway. This involves removing any boulders that stand in the way, and filling any potholes. The boulders are the things we have done that we should not have done; the potholes are the things we have failed to do which we obviously should have done. The more, as individuals, family or congregation, we are focused in this way, the less we will be overwhelmed by the commercialisation of Christmas.[1]

Personal exploration

Allow time for each person to ask themselves:

What does this mean in *my* situation?

Personal sharing

Invite those who are willing, to share any insight that came to them during that time of reflection.

---

1. *Celtic Daily Prayer*, p. 228

Group discussion

Slowly reread the quotation adding, perhaps, a few insights of your own – especially as you think of the advertisements with which we are bombarded at this time of year.

> Being ready for Christmas should mean that our thoughts are focused not just on letters and cards, shopping and presents,
> but on repentance,
> humbling
> and interior 'housecleaning.'
> John the Baptist warned his hearers to prepare a way for the Lord
> – to make a clear and level pathway.
> This involves removing any boulders that stand in the way,
> and filling any potholes.
> The boulders are the things we have done that we should not have done;
> the potholes are the things we have failed to do which we obviously should have done.
> The more, as individuals, family or congregation
> we are focused in this way,
> the less we will be overwhelmed by the commercialisation of Christmas.'[1]

Do you agree with these sentiments? If so, why? If not, why not?

Name some of the 'boulders' and 'potholes' that might need dealing with in the life of the individual, a small group like the one you are in at the moment, or the Church fellowship.

Worship time

- Light your candle if you have one. Or light three candles on the Advent wreath.

- Make sure your visual aid is central so that everyone can see it.

- Play a piece of music like the first part of 'Prepare the Way of the Lord' from the musical *Godspell*, or the hymn 'On Jordan's bank the Baptist's cry' or 'Ev'ry valley' from Handel's *Messiah*.

---

1. *Celtic Daily Prayer*, p. 228

- Use the following blessing. Let one person read the first line, then all join in with the refrain 'O come, O come, Emmanuel'.

> We are your waiting ones, O Lord.
> *O come, O come, Emmanuel.*
> We are your watching ones.
> *O come, O come, Emmanuel.*
> Our pathway through life is riddled with rocks.
> *O come, O come, Emmanuel.*
> Our road through life is riddled with ruts.
> *O come, O come, Emmanuel.*
> *and grant us the grace to prepare a place for you*
> *in our hearts.*

- Listen to 'Prayer for peace'.[1]

Preparing for next week

As Christmas cards arrive, look for pictures of Joseph and bring them with you to the next meeting. Meanwhile, ask whether one or two members of the group would make a collage of the pictures that have been brought this week.

---

1. This can be found on *River of Peace* CD or cassette published by Kevin Mayhew, or *Joy to the World* CD or cassette published by Eagle

Week 4

Fear-filled waiting

Visual focus

Place any pictures of Joseph that people have brought in the centre of the room.

Group preparation

- Listen to 'Mary's Song'.[1]

- Read aloud – all together – three times, the following verse in which God pleads with us:

  ### Be still and know that I am God.
  Psalm 46:10

- Respond to this invitation by becoming still.

- Tune into God's presence. Recognise that he is in the room with you now, greeting you, loving you, attentive to anything you want to say to him.

- Hand to him any anxieties or frustrations, tiredness or burdens that might prevent you from receiving what he wants to give you as a result of this time together.

- Quietly respond to his love.

Scripture focus

At this time of year, quite rightly, the spotlight is often placed on Mary, the young girl who so readily said yes when God's messenger broke the astonishing news that she had been chosen by God to become the mother of Jesus, the Messiah. This week, as well as focusing on Mary, we will also bring Joseph into the limelight. As we shall see, he has a great deal to teach us.

---

1. You will find this on the *Joy to the World* CD published by Eagle

The birth of Jesus Christ happened like this. When Mary was engaged to Joseph, just before their marriage, she was discovered to be pregnant – by the Holy Spirit. Whereupon Joseph, her future husband, who was a good man and did not want to see her disgraced, planned to break off the engagement quietly. But while he was turning the matter over in his mind an angel of the Lord appeared to him in a dream and said, 'Joseph, son of David, do not be afraid to take Mary as your wife! What she has conceived is conceived through the Holy Spirit, and she will give birth to a son, whom you will call Jesus ("the Saviour") for it is he who will save his people from their sins.'

Joseph woke up and did what the angel had told him. He married Mary, but had no intercourse with her until she had given birth to a son. And he gave him the name Jesus.

Matthew 1:18-21, 24-25 (J. B. Phillips)[1]

Comment

We are not told when Mary informed Joseph that she was pregnant. In fact, we are not even told whether or not Mary told him at all. Matthew seems to suggest that, somehow, Joseph 'discovered' Mary's secret. What we are told is that, when the secret was exposed, Joseph found himself in turmoil. On the one hand he was committed to Mary for life. (In those days and in that culture engagement was absolutely binding – as binding as marriage used to be in the West. The couple were even known as husband and wife even though they did not enjoy the rights of a married couple.) Matthew emphasises the fact that Joseph was a good man, so to break his pledge to Mary would have been almost unthinkable. At the same time, Joseph was a devout Jew – equally committed to the law of Moses. *That* law clearly dictates that, if a woman was found to have been unfaithful to her husband, she was to be stoned to death:

If a man happens to meet in a town a virgin pledged to be married and he sleeps with her, you shall take both of them to the gate of that town and stone them to death – the girl because she was in a town and did not scream for help, and the man because he violated another man's wife. You must purge this evil from among you.

Deuteronomy 22:23-24 (NIV)

---

1. J. B. Phillips, *The Gospels* (London: Geoffrey Bles, 1956)

Imagine the fear that fills Joseph's heart and mind as, right out of the blue, he wrestles with his lose-lose situation. If he does what the law demands, he condemns Mary to a cruel, humiliating death. How can he subject her to this when he loves her? On the other hand, the law of Moses left him with no choice. He *must* divorce Mary. If he refused, he risked losing the friendship of his family and neighbours, being excommunicated from the synagogue and, so he had been taught, of losing God also. Having weighed these options, unthinkable though it was, he chose to divorce Mary. To his credit, he decided to divorce her as quietly as possible. Legally there was only one way to do this. He would write a letter of divorce but not mention the reason why he was breaking off the relationship. He would not make the news public but simply hand this document to Mary in the presence of two witnesses rather than in public. If he made a public spectacle of her, she would be shamed and stoned to death on the outskirts of the village. Having made this difficult choice, he slept – only to have his sleep invaded by an angel who insisted that:

- He should not hesitate to marry Mary because she was speaking the truth when she claimed that her pregnancy had been Spirit-conceived.

- Mary would give birth to a son.

- Joseph himself had been chosen to play a unique part in the drama. Just as a father in the Middle East today names his child, Joseph was to name Mary's baby. In other words, he had been hand-picked to become the Messiah's surrogate father.

The Jewish theologian Alfred Edersheim highlights the reason why, for Joseph, this dream would have been highly significant:

A good dream was one of three things that were popularly rated as signs of God's favour. Conversely, another popular saying claimed that, 'If anyone sleeps seven days without dreaming (or rather remembering his dream for interpretation) call him wicked [that is] being unremembered by God.'[1]

Joseph was prompt in his obedience:

Joseph woke up and did what the angel had told him. He married Mary, but had no intercourse with her until she had given birth to a son. And he gave him the name Jesus.

Matthew 1:24-25 (J. B. Phillips)

---

1. Alfred Edersheim, *The Life and Times of Jesus the Messiah* (London: Longmans, Green and Co., 1901) p. 155

Personal exploration

Recall an occasion when, like Joseph, you had an almost impossible choice to make. Looking back, can you trace ways in which your dilemma became a time and space where grace was at work – that is, where God gave you the ability to do what was honourable and right; to do what he wanted you to do? If so, write a prayer of thanks to God. If, on the other hand, you recall a situation where you failed to act honourably, write a prayer telling God how you feel as you look back on that situation.

Personal sharing

Allow time for one or two people to share with the group the memories that came to them during that time of personal reflection.

Group discussion

- In her book *When the Heart Waits,* author Sue Monk Kidd claims that 'creativity flourishes not in certainty but in questions. Growth germinates not in tent dwelling but in upheaval.'[1] If Joseph could come to your group gathering, do you think he would agree with these claims? If so, why? If not, why not?

- Think of other occasions when Joseph acted equally promptly to the instructions given to him by God. What kind of person is it who places his or her life – present and future – into God's care in this way?

Worship time

- Light the four candles if you are using an Advent wreath.

- Play 'Joseph's song'.[2]

- Listen to the song again noticing the awe and gratitude Joseph is expressing.

- Invite one member of the group to read the following sentences that are printed in bold. Suggest that all the group should join in reading aloud the quotations from the Bible:

---

1. Sue Monk Kidd, *When the Heart Waits* (San Francisco: Harper San Francisco, 1990) p. 25
2. You will find this on *The Life* CD and cassette by Michael Card

Joseph was in a quandary. He didn't know what to do.

I pray to God . . .
and wait for what he'll say and do.
My life's on the line before God, my Lord,
waiting and watching till morning,
waiting and watching till morning.[1]

Joseph refused to make a hasty decision. He waited.

I wait for the Lord, my soul waits,
and in his word I put my hope.
My soul waits for the Lord
more than watchmen for the morning.[2]

Joseph was a good man.

Give me the grace, O God,
to maintain love and justice,
and to wait for you all my days.[3]

Joseph was in a lose-lose situation. He didn't know what was right and honourable.

Give me the grace, O God,
to believe that, when I don't know which way to turn
or what to do,
your Spirit will draw alongside me,
praying through me,
enlightening me,
guiding me,
working all the circumstances of my life
into something
Good.[4]

Joseph feared his own humiliation and the possible murder of Mary.

When I am afraid, O Lord Almighty,
I put my trust in you.
I trust in God and am not afraid;
I praise him for what he has promised.
What can a mere human being do to me?[5]

---

1. Psalm 25:5 (The Message)   4. Romans 8:25ff (The Message)
2. Psalm 130:6   5. Psalm 56:3-4 (Good News Bible)
3. Hosea 12:6

- Listen again to 'Joseph's Song' and/or 'As Joseph was awaking'.[1]

Preparing for next week

Look out this week for pictures of shepherds. You will probably find plenty on the Christmas cards that arrive. Bring one or two of your favourite pictures with you next week. Search, too, for pictures of and articles about society's outcasts.

---

1. You will find this on *The Saviour's Day* CD and cassette published by Eagle

Week 5

Patient waiting

Visual focus

Spread on the floor or on a table the pictures of shepherds and outcasts that you have brought to the group meeting.

Group preparation

* Listen to the Christmas Carol 'Silent night'.

* Try to imagine the deep-down stillness of that holy night by becoming silent and still yourself.

* In the silence, open your mind and heart and entire self to God, recognising that God is in the room with you, attentive to you, longing to reveal himself to you afresh.

* With hands and hearts and minds open, invite God to make his presence known and felt throughout this meeting and throughout the Christmas season.

* Pray that the following will be true for each member of the group as a result of this meeting:

We shall rest and we shall see,
We shall see and we shall know,
We shall know and we shall love,
We shall love and we shall praise.[1]

Scripture focus

Invite a member of the group to read aloud J. B. Phillips' paraphrase of Luke 2:8-20:

There were some shepherds living in the same part of the country, keeping guard throughout the night over their flock in the open fields. Suddenly an angel of the Lord stood by their side, the splendour of the Lord blazed around them, and they were terror-stricken. But the angel said to them:

'Do not be afraid! Listen, I bring you glorious news of great joy which is for every [person]. This very day, in David's town, a Saviour has

---

1. St Augustine

been born for you. He is Christ, the Lord. Let this prove it to you: you will find a baby, wrapped up and lying in a manger.'

And in a flash there appeared with the angel a vast host of the armies of heaven, praising God, saying:

'Glory to God in the highest heaven! Peace upon earth to [those] whom he loves!'

When the angels left them and went back into heaven, the shepherds said to each other:

'Now let us go straight to Bethlehem and see this event which the Lord has told us about.'

So they came as fast as they could and they found Mary and Joseph – and the baby lying in the manger. And when they had seen it, they told everybody what they had been told about the little child. And those who heard them were amazed at what the shepherds said. But Mary treasured all these things and turned them over in her mind. The shepherds went back to work, glorifying and praising God for everything that they had heard and seen, which had happened just as they had been told.[1]

Comment

At the time of Jesus' birth, shepherds were the outcasts of society. No law-abiding Jew would teach his son to become a shepherd because, according to the rabbis, it was impossible to keep the law *and* be a shepherd. The reason why the rabbis despised herdsmen in this way was that many of them deliberately drove their sheep onto other people's land and were therefore considered to be untrustworthy.[2] Because they were outcasts, many shepherds lived in caves outside the town of Bethlehem. Such caves can still be seen on the outskirts of Bethlehem today in what is sometimes known as 'The Shepherds' Field'.

Even though they were despised and rejected by society, the shepherds Luke refers to proved to be wonderfully responsive to God. There they were, doing what they did every night – protecting their sheep from sheep-stealers of various kinds. They never expected God to break into their ordinariness with his glory but when he did, they heard, they saw

---

1. J. B. Phillips, *The Gospels* (London: Geoffrey Bles, 1956)
2. Here I am drawing on the insights of Professor Kenneth Bailey in *Finding the Lost* (St Louis: Concordia 1992) p. 65

and they so trusted the message of the angel that, immediately, they obeyed. So, as soon as the angelic choir disappeared, they rushed off to Bethlehem to discover for themselves the scene the angel spokesman had described for them. I like the way Walter Wangerin describes the scene. Try to picture it for yourself as you read this short excerpt from his book *The Book of God*:

By midnight the fires of the three shepherds had collapsed into sparks and red embers. Simon and the two others who joined flocks and shared the long nightwatch had also subsided into silence . . . Simon had gone to lie among the sheep for warmth, but he wasn't sleeping. He was gazing thoughtfully upward and enjoying the periodic huffings and sighs of the larger ewes.

All at once the stars began to explode.

Simon leaped to his feet.

The sheep stumbled up, bleating and running back to the stone walls.

The stars – in tens, and then in tens of thousands – were flashing like white fires in the black sky! They began to move.

Like burning bees, like a great whirling swarm of bees, the stars were crossing heaven from the east to the west.

Simon stood immobilised. Even the sheep were fixed in attitudes of awful fear.

Between the glorious motion of heaven and the dark earth below, there now appeared a single, endless pillar of pure white fire.

And the fire spoke, and Simon understood what it said.

The fire cried, 'Don't be afraid!'

No, *not* the fire – but a figure within the fire! The brilliant form of a human, smooth and huge and very beautiful, his feet upon the mountains.

An angel of the Lord!

The angel said, 'I bring good news of great joy which shall come to all the people. For to you is born this night in the city of David a Saviour who is Christ the Lord! And this will be a sign for you: you will find a baby wrapped in swaddling cloths and lying in a manger.'

Suddenly that swarm of the fiery heavenly host swooped down and filled the lower skies, praising God and singing:

Glory to God in the highest!
And on earth peace to the people with whom he is pleased!

How long the enormous chorus lasted, Simon did not know. The air itself was the music of these angels. When they withdrew again to heaven, and the night was dark, Simon thought he could hear nothing but what he had heard, *Gloria*, still ringing in his ears; and he thought he was blinded to the common things around him, stone and sheep, his companions and his own hand.

But the older man that had been snoring whispered, 'Simon?' – and Simon heard that very well.

'Simon,' said the shepherd, 'did you see that, too?'

Simon gazed solemnly at his friend and under common starlight nodded.

The third shepherd joined them.

The old man gaped at them both and whispered, 'And did you hear what the angel said to us?'

Simon nodded.

'It was the Lord,' the old man said. 'It was the Lord who made these things known to us.'

Simon stepped out of the sheepfold and carefully closed the gate. He pushed the gate of the goats, testing its latch, then he began to walk up the northwest slope of the valley. The other men joined him. At the crest of the hill Simon broke into a run. Faster and faster he ran, until he was flying. His heart was very light. His legs were tireless. His eye saw the fires of Bethlehem immediately, and he kept his sight there while they grew to meet his nearness.

Simon did not even pause at the edge of town. He sailed the narrow streets knowing nothing, yet trusting his foot to find the right place. And it did . . . [When the shepherds saw Mary, Joseph and the Christ-child,] Simon sighed. The air went from him in a long and inarticulate sound:

'A Saviour! The Messiah . . .'

'Mother,' Simon said, 'your baby is the most beautiful baby I have ever seen. As soft as the nose of a lamb.'[1]

Having found and seen and worshipped the newborn king, the shepherds returned to their field, glorifying and praising God *and* spreading the good news of the Saviour's birth far and near.

Personal exploration

Try to put yourself into the sandals of one of the shepherds. See the stars, listen to the message of the angel, run with the shepherds to the place where Jesus was lying in a manger, worship the newborn Messiah. Discover what it is that you want to do and say.

Personal sharing

Invite members of the group to share what they saw and heard and did and felt when they found Mary and Joseph and Jesus.

Group discussion

- When Jesus was born, God chose to reveal that fact to the outcasts of society because he longs that 'the poor' might be drawn to him. Recalling God's compassion for 'the poor', if Jesus were to be born this evening into our culture, what section of society might receive a visit from a choir of angels?

- In the book we referred to last week, *When the Heart Waits*, Sue Monk Kidd describes a life-changing encounter she once had with someone who startled her with these words:

    When you're waiting, you're *not* doing nothing. You're doing the most important something there is. You're allowing your soul to grow up. If you can't be still and wait, you can't become what God created you to be.[2]

    If the person had said that to you when you were being forced to wait, how might you have responded?

---

1. Walter Wangerin, *The Book of God* (Oxford: Lion, 1996) pp. 597-599
2. Sue Monk Kidd, *op. cit.*, p. 22

Worship time

One reason why some people find it helpful to light a candle as they come into God's presence is that the lighted candle can symbolise Christ, the Light of the World. If members of the group find it helpful to worship by candlelight, light a candle before you begin this section.

- Focusing on the Light of the World, listen to the aria 'There were shepherds abiding in the fields' from Handel's *Messiah*. As you listen, recall the things that have been read and said and shared during the meeting and ponder the mysterious way in which Jesus made his entry into the world.

- Recalling the way the shepherds *hurried* into Bethlehem to see for themselves the baby the angels described, say the following prayer together:

I open the stable door;
I kneel before the infant;
I worship with the shepherds;
I adore the Christ child.
I give my love with Mary and Joseph;
I wonder at the 'Word made flesh'.
I am aware of the love of God;
I sing glory with the angels . . .
I receive the living Lord;
I hold him in my hands;
I go on my way rejoicing,
glorifying and praising God.
David Adam[1]

Preparing for next week

Look through your Christmas cards or catalogues or Christmas books for pictures of the wise men *en route* for Bethlehem maybe, or presenting their gifts to Jesus. Bring your favourite pictures with you next week.

---

1. David Adam, quoted *Celtic Daily Prayer*, p. 231

Week 6

Dedicated watching

Visual focus

For many Christians, 6 January is a very special day. On this day the Orthodox Church celebrates the birth of Jesus while many Christians in the West celebrate the Feast of the Epiphany – that is, the arrival in Bethlehem of the magi. So this week we place the spotlight on this curious, thrilling chapter of the unfolding saga of the events that surrounded Jesus' birth. To help the group to visualise the events on which we place the spotlight today, place in the centre of the room the pictures of the magi that members of the group have brought. Or, if you have been using a nativity set as a visual aid, let the main focus be Mary and Joseph and Jesus but gradually bring the wise men and their camels closer and closer to the holy family.

Group preparation

- Listen to or sing the carol 'O come, all ye faithful'.

- Be still for a few minutes and gradually become aware of the internal clutter you bring to the meeting: the encouragements, excitements and successes; the disappointments, failures and pressures . . .

- Try to recognise where God was present in all that has happened in your life. Then write a prayer telling God what you hope for from this meeting. Ask yourself whether you would like to read your prayer aloud when the opportunity arises. If not, why not? If so, why?

Scripture focus

Now read this modern paraphrase of Matthew 2:2-8:

> After Jesus was born in Bethlehem village, Judah territory – this was during Herod's kingship – a band of scholars arrived in Jerusalem from the East. They asked around, 'Where can we find and pay homage to the newborn King of the Jews? We observed a star in the eastern sky that signaled his birth. We're on pilgrimage to worship him.'
>
> When word of their inquiry got to Herod, he was terrified – and not Herod alone, but most of Jerusalem as well. Herod lost no time. He gathered all the high priests and religion scholars in the city together and asked, 'Where is the Messiah supposed to be born?'

They told him, 'Bethlehem, in Judah's land,
   no longer bringing up the rear.
From you will come the leader
   who will shepherd-rule my people, my Israel.'

Herod then arranged a secret meeting with the scholars from the East. Pretending to be as devout as they were, he got them to tell him exactly when the birth-announcement star appeared. Then he told them the prophecy about Bethlehem, and said, 'Go find this child. Leave no stone unturned. As soon as you find him, send word and I'll join you at once in your worship.'

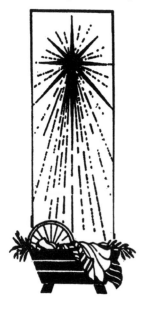

Instructed by the king, they set off. Then the star appeared again, the same star they had seen in the eastern skies. It led them on until it hovered over the place of the child. They could hardly contain themselves: They were in the right place! They had arrived at the right time!

They entered the house and saw the child in the arms of Mary, his mother. Overcome, they kneeled and worshipped him. Then they opened their luggage and presented gifts: gold, frankincense, myrrh.

In a dream, they were warned not to report back to Herod. So they worked out another route, left the territory without being seen, and returned to their own country.
Matthew 2:2-13 (The Message)

Personal exploration

This passage of Scripture is old yet ever new. Before the group starts to unpack it, let each of the group members answer the following question in their hearts:

- Did anything in particular strike me as I read that modern translation of a familiar story? If so, what was it: a word, a phrase, a sentence, a word picture, a memory, a particular part of the story?

Let it rise to the surface of your mind and heart for a few minutes. Savour it. Tell God how you feel about this insight that has made an impact on you. Then, remembering that prayer comes from your heart and not your head, write another prayer to God based on what you have seen and heard and felt.

Personal sharing

Invite individuals to spell out what it was that moved or impressed or made an impact on them if they would like to. Remember, though, that this is a time for sharing and not for discussion!

Group discussion

Read carefully the following definitions of the word 'worship'.

- Worship is always more or less deeply coloured by mystery.
- Worship is a devoted proclamation of the splendour, the wonder and the beauty of God.
- Worship consists in rejoicing in the beauty of God.
- Worship is the opening of our heart to God's love.
- Worship is the surrender of our will to God's purpose.
- Worship is adoration – the most selfless emotion of which we are capable.

How would you define worship?

Invite the group now to divide into sub-groups of three people in each group. Let each sub-group appoint a spokesperson. Then challenge each group to create a short, sharp, succinct definition of the word 'worship'. Place a time limit on the discussion. When the time is up, invite each spokesperson to read the group's definition.

Comment: a pilgrimage of worship

Last year, when I read the passage of Scripture we are focusing on to a group of people, the phrase that seemed to beckon me to itself was this: 'We're on pilgrimage to worship him.' Here, we trace the pilgrimage the magi made.

- These men were almost certainly astrologers – people who read the language of the stars. While they were going about their ordinary work, God broke into their lives.

- Many now believe that 'the star' the magi saw was the planet Jupiter that shines as brightly by day as by night.[1]

- The magi knew enough about the language of the sky to know that this amazing spectacle heralded the birth of a very special king – the Messiah. They would have known about the prophecies foretelling the Messiah's birth through Jews who lived in their part of the world.

- The sight of the star awakened in them the desire to go to welcome into the world the newborn Messiah.

- Some believe these men lived in Persia. Others suggest that they came from Iraq or Iran or Oman. We shall never know the precise country of their origin. What we do know is that their journey was long and difficult and tiring. Yet their watching was so dedicated that they persevered – and were rewarded.

For further discussion

- Picture the magi setting out on their journey. How do you sense they might be feeling?

- Picture them *on* the journey. What difficulties and dangers do you think they encountered?

> The magi searched in Jerusalem.
> They found the baby in Bethlehem.
> They worshipped.
> They heard God speak to them.
> They obeyed.
> They returned – the same, yet strangely changed.

- Try to imagine how they felt as they presented their gifts to the baby Messiah. Make a list of their emotions.

- Picture Mary and Joseph as the magi entered their home to present their gifts. How do you imagine *they* felt?

Worship time

- Light the candle if you are using one.

---

1. If you have access to the video of the BBC television programme, *Son of God*, Jeremy Bowen explains this theory in detail. The subject is also covered in the book *Son of God* by Angela Tilby, published by Hodder & Stoughton

- Invite someone to read the definitions of worship that appear on page 61.

- Invite someone else to read the definitions of worship that the group have provided.

- Listen to the song 'Like a candle flame'.[1]

- Say the following prayer together:

Christ as a light
illumine and guide me!
Christ as a shield overshadow and cover me!
Christ be under me!
Christ be over me!
Christ be beside me,
on left hand and right!
Christ be before me, behind me, about me!
Christ, this day, be within and without me!

St Patrick

- Listen to the song 'Jesus is our joy'.[2]

- Say together:

This only do I ask
of your extreme kindness –
that you convert me
wholly to you
and you allow nothing
to prevent me
from wending my way to you.

St Augustine

Preparing for next week

During the week, buy or make a gift that costs just 50 pence or less; a gift that you could give to any member of the group. Wrap your gift before you come to the next meeting.

---

1. This song may be found on *The Graham Kendrick Collection* CD and cassette published by Kevin Mayhew
2. You will find this song on the CD and cassette *Fire of Love* by Margaret Rizza, published by Kevin Mayhew

Week 7

Worshipful watching

Visual focus

Place the gifts that you have brought in a pile either on the floor in the middle of the room or on a table where all can see them. They will be a visible reminder that the subject of today's session is *giving gifts*.

Group preparation

- Listen to the hymn 'Brightest and best of the sons of the morning' or 'We three kings of Orient are'.

- Look back over the Christmas period and recall some of the good things that have happened for you. In the silence thank God for them as you recall that every good gift and every perfect gift comes from him.

- Tune in to the presence of God – Immanuel – *God with us* – God with you in this meeting at this moment.

- Tune in, too, to God's loving attentiveness to each member of the group.

- Write a prayer telling God what it is that you are hoping for from this meeting.

Scripture focus

The wise men listened to the king and then went on their way to Bethlehem. And now the star, which they had seen in the east, went in front of them as they travelled until at last it shone immediately above the place where the little child lay. The sight of the star filled them with indescribable joy.

So they went into the house and saw the little child with his mother Mary. And they fell on their knees and worshipped him. Then they opened their treasures and presented him with gifts – gold, incense and myrrh.

Matthew 2:9-11 (J. B. Phillips)[1]

Comment

We are given no clue about how long it took the wise men to make the journey from 'the east' to Bethlehem. What we are given is a moving

---

1. J. B. Phillips, *The Gospels* (London: Geoffrey Bles, 1956)

account of their reaction when, at long last, they caught their first glimpse of the Christ-child. Picture the scene as we place the spotlight on the moment of encounter they had been waiting for and longing for:

They went into the house and saw the little child with his mother Mary. And they fell on their knees and worshipped him.

The picture that Matthew paints here reminds me of one Christmas Eve when my husband and I attended a very special Communion service. The service started soon after 11pm. In front of the chapel where the service was being held, someone had placed two waiting figurines. One was Joseph, the other was Mary. On the stroke of midnight, after we had sung our carols, listened to the age-old but ever-new story of the birth of Jesus and received the bread and wine, the door of the chapel was opened and, with great reverence, pride and joy, a member of the congregation carried in the baby with both her hands – high in the air for all to see – then gently laid the child in the manger that had been placed beside Mary and Joseph. The chapel seemed to be so filled with awe that almost everyone knelt in wonder, love and silent praise.

Matthew seems to suggest that the sight of the Saviour of the world wrapped in human flesh produced a similar response from the magi who, like men in that part of the world today, are unafraid to express their deep-down feelings.

Having first given Jesus the gift he longs for most from each of us – the gift of wonder, love and praise – the wise men then opened their treasures: gold, frankincense and myrrh. Gold is a treasure indeed – costly even in that part of the world – so a gift worthy of a king. Frankincense is gum from a tree which, according to Jeremiah 51:8, has healing properties. When burned, frankincense fills the air with a sweet, pungent smell, which is why it is still burned today, not only in the *souks*[1] but in

---

1. The bazaars or markets

homes also – particularly when a host and hostess wish to welcome a special guest. Myrrh is also an aromatic gum whose oil was used by beauticians (see Esther 2:12), for medicinal purposes when eaten or mixed with wine (see Mark 15:23), and for embalming the dead (see John 19:39-40).

Personal exploration

- Close your eyes and try to picture the wise men unpacking their treasures and presenting them to Mary and Joseph and Jesus.

- Now ask yourself, 'If *I* had had the privilege of visiting the newborn Jesus, what might I have brought? And where would I have placed it?'

Personal sharing

Some members of the group might value the opportunity to share with everyone what it is that they would have brought for the baby – and where they would have placed it. Make time for this sharing before the group discussion.

Group discussion

- The wise men gave God another treasure that we have not yet mentioned. One Christmas carol calls it 'the gold of obedience'. When God used a dream urging the wise men to return to their homeland via a different route from the one they used to reach Bethlehem, the visitors from the east obeyed. What might have happened if they had disobeyed?

- In his book *The Story of the Christ Child*, Leon Morris writes:

  So often when we present our gifts to the Christ we do not open up our treasures. We give to him, not the things we value highly, but those that we can most easily afford, whether it be in terms of money, or time, or companionships, or our talents, or whatever it be. We give our second best. We still need to learn that the gifts that cost us nothing are worth precisely what they cost.[1]

  Do you think that Leon Morris' claim is accurate? If so, why do you feel that way? How can we ensure that we do not fall into this trap ourselves?

---

1. Leon Morris, *The Story of the Christ Child* (London: Marshall, Morgan and Scott, 1960) p. 122

Worship time

- Light a candle if you are using one to help you turn from discussion to worship.
- Listen to the song 'Father, never was your love so near'.[1]
- Say the following prayer together:

O Lord our God,
grant us the grace
to desire you with our whole heart,
that so desiring we may see and find you,
and so finding you
may love you,
and loving you
may hate those sins
from which you have redeemed us.
St Anselm

- Listen to 'The giving song'.[2]
- Play this joyful song again, joining in if you can. While you do this, pick up the gift that you brought with you to the meeting and give it to the person on your left.
- When everyone has opened their gift, say the following prayer together:

May the love and light of God
scatter the darkness from us
and guide our feet into the way of peace.
And may the blessing of God Almighty,
the Father,
the Son
and the Holy Spirit
be with us as we go
and remain with us
now and always.

---

1. This song has been recorded on *The Graham Kendrick Christmas Collection* CD published by Kevin Mayhew
2. This song has been recorded on *The Graham Kendrick Christmas Collection* CD published by Kevin Mayhew

Preparing for next week

Bring to the next and final meeting a sturdy cardboard circle that is about four inches in diameter and that has a hole in the middle that is large enough to hold a small candle.

Invite someone to volunteer to bring a packet of such small candles with them next week so that one can be given to each member of the group.

Week 8

Persistent watching

Visual focus

Candles play an important part in today's meeting, so, if at all possible, place a large candle in a prominent position in the room where the group is meeting, ensuring that everyone can see it. Light this candle at the beginning of the meeting and place around it the smaller candles that have been slotted into their cardboard 'cradles' – but don't light the smaller candles yet!

Group preparation

- As you gaze at the lighted candle, listen to the song 'You are the light'.[1]

- Be aware of any darkness that you are in touch with: darkness within your family or neighbourhood or church; darkness hitting the news headlines; darkness within yourself. Ask God to shine his light into bleak and black places.

- Be aware, too, of any worries or fears or other emotions that might prevent you from entering into all that God wants to give you during this meeting. Do what Peter invites us to do in 1 Peter 5:7. Hand your burdens to God trusting that he so cares about you that he will take the burdens from you, at least for the duration of this meeting; then he will give you the grace to cope with them.

- Tune into the fact that love is what God is. With your heart and hands and mind open, receive that love into yourself.

Comment

For countless Christians throughout the world 2 February is a very important date in the diary because, on that day, they recall that Christmas Day was 40 days ago. The fortieth day after the birth of Jesus proved to be an unforgettable one for Joseph and Mary. On that day, they took their baby to the Temple in Jerusalem. They did this for several reasons. One was that the law required it. A woman was considered to be unclean

---

1. This song, sometimes known as 'Enfold me in your love', has been recorded on the CD and cassette *Chants and Songs* by Margaret Rizza, published by Kevin Mayhew

for 40 days after the birth of a baby boy so, during these 40 days, she was not permitted to take part in any religious ceremony or to enter the temple. At the end of the 40 days, though, she was required to bring to the temple as an offering either a lamb and a pigeon, or, if she could not afford a lamb, two pigeons or two doves. Neither the mother nor her child was believed to be under divine protection until these ceremonies prescribed by the Levitical law had been performed (Leviticus 12:2, 6). Joseph and Mary brought 'the offering of the poor' – two small doves – to the Temple to comply with this law. Another reason why they came was to fulfil another part of the same law – the clause that insisted that every male child should be offered back to God.

Scripture focus

Luke describes in graphic detail what happened to the holy family on this first visit to the Temple together. Invite a member of the group to read the following paraphrase of Luke 2:22ff *slowly* and clearly – not just once but twice. Before the reading, invite members of the group to listen to the familiar words carefully, expecting a word or a phrase, a sentence or a pen picture to beckon them to itself. Encourage them then to turn 'their' word or phrase or sentence or pen picture over and over in their minds while the reading continues.

> When the days stipulated by Moses for purification were complete, [Mary and Joseph] took Jesus up to Jerusalem to offer him to God as commanded in God's law: 'Every male who opens the womb shall be a holy offering to God,' and also to sacrifice the 'pair of doves or two young pigeons' prescribed in God's Law.
>
> In Jerusalem at the time, there was a man, Simeon by name, a good man, a man who lived in the prayerful expectancy of help for Israel. And the Holy Spirit was on him. The Holy Spirit had shown him that he would see the Messiah of God before he died. Led by the Spirit, he entered the Temple. As the parents of the child Jesus brought him in to carry out the rituals of the law, Simeon took him into his arms and blessed God:
>
> 'God, you can now release your servant;
>   release me in peace as you promised.
> With my own eyes I've seen your salvation;
>   it's now out in the open for everyone to see:
> A God-revealing light to the non-Jewish nations,
>   and of glory for your people Israel.'

SIMEON TOOK THE CHILD JESUS IN HIS ARMS AND PRAISED GOD

Jesus' father and mother were speechless with surprise at these words. Simeon went on to bless them, and said to Mary his mother,

'This child marks both the failure
   and the recovery of many in Israel.
A figure misunderstood and contradicted –
   the pain of a sword-thrust through you –
But the rejection will force honesty,
   as God reveals who they really are.'

Anna the prophetess was also there . . . She was by now a very old woman. She had been married seven years and a widow for eighty-four. She never left the Temple area, worshipping night and day with her fastings and prayers. At the very time Simeon was praying, she showed up, broke into an anthem of praise to God, and talked about the child to all who were waiting expectantly for the freeing of Jerusalem.

When [Joseph and Mary] finished everything required by God in the law, they returned to Galilee and their own town, Nazareth. There the child grew strong in body and wise in spirit. And the grace of God was on him.

Luke2:22-40 (The Message)

Personal exploration

When this reading has been read at least twice, remain still and silent for several minutes so that you can savour 'your' word or phrase or sentence by turning it over and over in your mind until the truth of it trickles from your head into your heart.

Allow several minutes for this to take place. Don't be in a hurry to move on!

When you are ready, write a prayer to God out of the experience you have just had.

Personal sharing

When members of the group have finished writing their prayers, leave time for each person first to share with the person next to them the word or phrase or sentence or pen picture that drew them to itself. When everyone has had the opportunity to do this, ask whether anyone would like to share 'their' word or phrase or sentence with everyone in the group. If they want to explain *why* they believe they were touched by these words or picture, give them the space to do so.

Again, leave plenty of time for this sharing. There is no need to rush.

Group discussion

The group may need to divide into two for this part of the meeting. Appoint a spokesperson for each group so that that person can feed their mini-group's ideas and findings back to the *whole* group. One group can then respond to this question:

1. What do we learn about Simeon from this passage of Scripture? How can we become more like him?

The other group can answer the following question:

2. What do we learn about Anna from this passage of Scripture? How can we become more like her?

Worship time

- At the beginning of this time of worship that brings the Advent/ Christmas/Epiphany season to a close, invite each member of the group to pick up one of the small candles surrounded by the protective cardboard circle. Then one member of the group – perhaps the host or hostess – should light their small candle from the larger candle in the centre of the room. This member of the group then turns to the person next to them and lights that person's candle – and so on until all the candles are alight, illustrating Simeon's description of Jesus: *A God-revealing light for all nations.*

- Imagine Christ's glory and light filling the room, your heart and the world as you enjoy the glow of the candles and listen to the song 'In the Lord is my joy and salvation'.[1]

---

1. This song is recorded on the *Fire of Love* CD and cassette by Margaret Rizza, published by Kevin Mayhew

- Say the following together:

  Six weeks ago, we focused on your Second Coming,
  Jesus, Saviour of the world.
  Forty days ago, we celebrated your birth.

  In our group meetings we have been reminded that your calling
  was bitter-sweet. Sweet because, through your outpoured love, you
  would win many hearts. Bitter because by many you were to be
  rejected in such a way that you would be known as 'the man of
  sorrows', the one who was acquainted with grief.

  We look back on the mystery of your birth with gratitude.

  May all that we have shared together
  prepare us for the contemplation of that even greater mystery:
  your death and resurrection.

  As you prepared us to celebrate Advent and Christmas,
  the Epiphany and the Presentation in the Temple,
  now prepare us to journey *with you* –

  through Lent
  into your Passion and Death
  through Easter
  to your Ascension into heaven
  and on into Pentecost.

  As we give thanks for all that we have learned and shared
  in our time together as a group,
  we ask that you may be born again in us
  and glorified through who we are.

  We ask, too, that *your* eyes may ever hold us,
  your love ever draw us,
  your glance ever enfold us
  each night and each day,
  from now into eternity.[1]

- Listen to 'A blessing',[2] praying silently for each member of the group
  as you do so. Finally, extinguish your candle.

---

1. The four lines before the last line are an adaptation of words found on a Carmelite Christmas card
2. This song is recorded on the *Fire of Love* CD and cassette by Margaret Rizza, published by Kevin Mayhew